D0700187

JUN 1 4 2013

MEASURING TIME: THE CLOCK

By Julia Vogel • Illustrated by Luanne Marten

SAN DIEGO PUBLIC LIBRARY

LA JOLLA

The Child's World

Published by The Child's World®
1980 Lookout Drive • Mankato, MN 56003-1705
800-599-READ • www.childsworld.com

Acknowledgments
The Child's World®: Mary Berendes, Publishing Director
The Design Lab: Cover and interior design
Amnet: Cover and interior production
Red Line Editorial: Editorial direction

Photo credits
Dreamstime, cover, 1; Shutterstock Images, cover, 1, 2, 5, 6, 11, 16, 23; Alex Hubenov/
Shutterstock Images, 9; Valery Shanin/Shutterstock Images, 12; Cliff Parnell/iStockphoto, 19

Copyright © 2013 by The Child's World®
All rights reserved. No part of this book may be reproduced or utilized in
any form or by any means without written permission from the publisher.

ISBN 9781614732822
LCCN 2012933671

Printed in the United States of America
Mankato, MN
July 2012
PA02121

ABOUT THE AUTHOR
Award-winning author Julia Vogel spent hours and hours studying biology in college and forestry in graduate school. Julia's favorite times are spent reading, writing, or hiking with her husband and four children.

ABOUT THE ILLUSTRATOR
Luanne Marten has been drawing for a long time. She earned a bachelor's degree in art and design from the University of Kansas. She enjoys spending her spare minutes and hours reading and her free days traveling.

TABLE OF CONTENTS

Keeping Track of Time

Busy kids need to keep track of time. What do you keep track of? When school starts? How much longer you get to play outside for recess?

Calendars measure long periods of time such as days, weeks, and months. You also need a way to measure shorter amounts of time. A clock is used to measure seconds, minutes, and hours.

Knowing how to tell time on a clock is an important skill.

Before clocks, the rising sun signaled the start of the day.

Rising with the Sun

The earliest farmers did not need to know exact times of day or night. They woke at sunrise and worked in the daylight. They fell asleep around sunset.

These people noticed the sun moved from one side of the sky to the other throughout the day. The sun's position helped them make a good guess of the time.

The Sundial

People then put the sun to work measuring time. Shadows cast by the sun change as the day goes on. People learned to use a blade shaped like a triangle to make a shadow. The shadow pointed in different directions throughout the day. Marks on the ground where it pointed told the time. The shadow clock was called a **sundial**. Sundials let people divide the day into smaller bits of time called hours.

HOURS IN A DAY
People figured out that a full day is 24 hours long. This is how long it takes Earth to spin around once.

A sundial tells the time on a sunny day.

The Hourglass

Around the 1300s, a new timekeeping tool was created: the **hourglass**. Sailors used hourglasses on ships to keep track of how long they stood watch. Sundials did not really work on the water.

BOARD GAMES
People still use sand-filled timers. You might use one to time turns in a board game.

In an hourglass, sand trickles from the top bulb to the bottom bulb.

Bells in the towers let people know when each hour passed.

The Clock

Around the same time hourglasses were first used, inventors created new time-measuring machines called clocks. Towers had bells with a clock inside. The machine rang a bell on each hour. The bell called people to church and town meetings. People began to talk of times of day based on bell rings from the clock. "One bell of the clock" became "one o'clock."

Minutes and Seconds

Clocks got better with time. Hours on the clock were split into 60 minutes. Minutes were split into 60 seconds. People all around the world use the same time measuring **units** of hours, minutes, and seconds.

TIME IT
How long is a minute to you? Ask someone to time you while you stand on one foot. Does it seem like a long or a short time? How long is a second to you? Ask someone to time you while you count your heartbeats. How many times does your heart beat in ten seconds?

Kids around the world use clocks during the day and night.

clock face

hour hand

minute hand

second hand

A wall clock

THE THREE HANDS
It takes 12 hours for the hour hand to move around the clock face. It takes 60 minutes for the minute hand to move around the clock face. It takes 60 seconds for the second hand to make a full turn.

Telling Time

Now you can learn to tell time. Clocks with faces usually have numbers written in a circle from 1 to 12. They also have two hands. The short one is the hour hand. The long one is the minute hand. Sometimes clocks have second hands, too.

To tell the hour, look where the hour hand is pointing. To tell minutes, look where the minute hand is pointing.

Analog and Digital

For centuries inventors have kept improving clocks. You might have a clock on the wall of your classroom, on the stove, and in your family's car. You may even have a small clock that you wear on your wrist. It's a watch!

Some of the clocks and watches have faces with hands and numbers. These are **analog clocks**. Many clocks have numbers that are always changing. They do not have hands. These are **digital clocks**. On a digital clock, the numbers on the left of the colon (:) tell the hour. The numbers on the right tell the minutes.

Wearing a watch helps you keep track of time when you are on the go.

Other Ways to Say the Time

Sometimes people tell time by saying how many minutes it is until a certain hour. They might say it is "ten to two." That means the time is ten minutes until 2:00, or 1:50.

Some minutes on the clock have two ways of saying things. These times work by splitting the clock into four equal parts, or quarters. At 2:15, you can say it is "quarter after two." When the time is at 6:30, you can say it is "half past six."

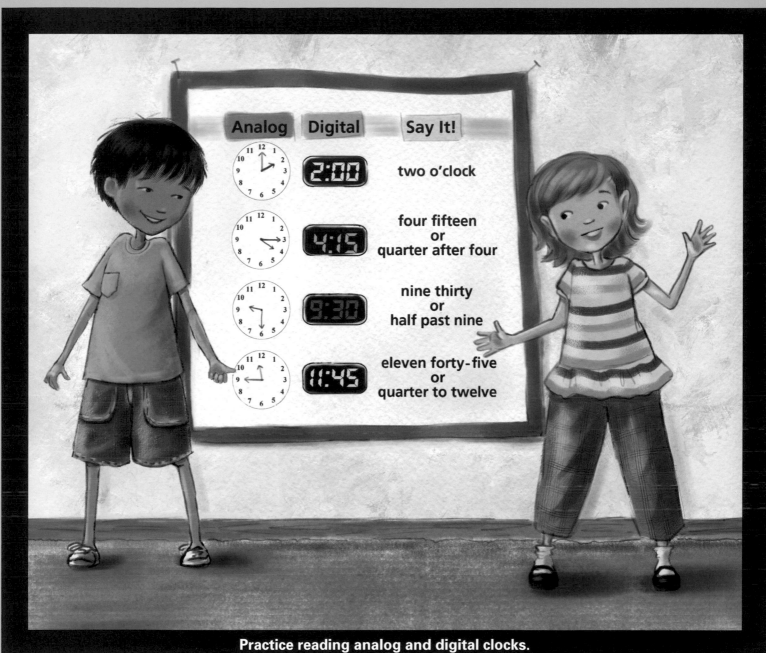

Practice reading analog and digital clocks.

Terrific Timekeeping

Is your clock on your computer, wrist, or wall? Wherever you keep it, use it to keep track of the time and all your activities. What time does school start? When is soccer today?

You can answer these questions and more. Get your clock and start measuring!

ADDING AND SUBTRACTING
Telling time is a good way to practice math. If it is 2:00 now, and your cousin is coming over for dinner at 6:00, how long until he arrives? Subtract the hours: six minus two. Your cousin is coming over in four hours!

Practice telling time until you're a terrific timekeeper.

Glossary

analog clocks (AN-uh-lawg KLAHKS): Analog clocks are tools for measuring time with hands pointing to hours and minutes. Analog clocks have faces.

digital clocks (DIJ-i-tuhl KLAHKS): Digital clocks are tools for measuring time that show time in numbers. Digital clock numbers are always changing.

hourglass (OUR-glass): An hourglass is a sand-filled tool for measuring time. An hourglass is sometimes used in board games.

sundial (SUHN-dye-uhl): A sundial is a tool that tells time by casting a shadow from the sun. A sundial is only good for telling time during sunny days.

units (YOU-nits): Units are standard amounts used to measure. Hours, minutes, and seconds are units of time.

Books

Harris, Trudy. *The Clock Struck One: A Time-Telling Tale*. Minneapolis, MN: Millbrook Press, 2009.

Maestro, Betsy. *The Story of Clocks and Calendars*. New York: HarperCollins, 2004.

Williams, Brian. *Measuring Time*. Mankato, MN: Smart Apple Media, 2003.

Web Sites

Visit our Web site for links about measuring time with clocks: **childsworld.com/links**

Note to Parents, Teachers, and Librarians: We routinely verify our Web links to make sure they are safe and active sites. So encourage your readers to check them out!

Index